CH

Big Challenges
that Animals Face

Bobbie Kalman

🜋 Crabtree Publishing Company
www.crabtreebooks.com

Big
Science Ideas

Created by Bobbie Kalman

For our friends Andrew Porteus and Louise Waldie,
who make challenging car rallies easy and fun

Author
Bobbie Kalman

Photo research
Bobbie Kalman

Editors
Kathy Middleton
Crystal Sikkens

Design
Bobbie Kalman
Katherine Berti

Print and production coordinator
Katherine Berti

Photographs
Digital Vision: page 21 (top left)
iStockphoto: page 24
Thinkstock: page 6
Wikimedia Commons:
    Kent Backman: page 11 (top right);
    Quyet Le: page 13; NOAA: page 25 (bottom);
    U.S. Fish and Wildlife Service: page 25 (top);
    USFWS Mountain-Prairie: page 28 (bottom);
    Lhb1239: page 29 (top)
Shutterstock.com:
    KY CHO: page 1;
    Carlos Amarillo: page 5 (top right);
    think4photop: page 7 (bottom);
    Sergey Uryadnikov: page 14 (top);
    Matyas Rehak: page 19 (middle);
    Mike Price: page 22; Serenethos: page 23 (top);
    Jamesbox: page 27 (bottom)
Covers and other photos by Shutterstock

Library and Archives Canada Cataloguing in Publication

Kalman, Bobbie, author
    Big challenges that animals face / Bobbie Kalman.

(Big science ideas)
Includes index.
Issued in print and electronic formats.
ISBN 978-0-7787-2781-1 (bound).--ISBN 978-0-7787-2789-7 (paperback).--
ISBN 978-1-4271-8096-4 (html)

    1. Wildlife conservation--Juvenile literature. 2. Endangered
species--Juvenile literature. 3. Habitat conservation--Juvenile literature.
I. Title. II. Series: Kalman, Bobbie. Big science ideas.

QH75.K34 2016   j333.95'416   C2015-908704-X
                                                    C2015-908705-8

Library of Congress Cataloging-in-Publication Data

Names: Kalman, Bobbie, author.
Title: Big challenges that animals face / Bobbie Kalman.
Description: New York, New York : Crabtree Publishing Company,
    [2016] | Series: Big science ideas | Includes index. | Description based
    on print version record and CIP data provided by publisher; resource
    not viewed.
Identifiers: LCCN 2015045728 (print) | LCCN 2015044808 (ebook) |
    ISBN 9781427180964 (electronic HTML) | ISBN 9780778727811
    (reinforced library binding : alk. paper) | ISBN 9780778727897 (pbk. :
    alk. paper)
Subjects: LCSH: Wildlife conservation--Juvenile literature. | Endangered
    species--Juvenile literature. | Habitat conservation--Juvenile literature.
Classification: LCC QH75 (print) | LCC QH75 .K34 2016 (ebook) | DDC
    333.95/416--dc23
LC record available at http://lccn.loc.gov/2015045728

Crabtree Publishing Company

www.crabtreebooks.com   1-800-387-7650

Printed in Canada/022016/IH20151223

Published in Canada
Crabtree Publishing
616 Welland Ave.
St. Catharines, Ontario
L2M 5V6

Published in the United States
Crabtree Publishing
PMB 59051
350 Fifth Avenue, 59th Floor
New York, New York 10118

Published in the United Kingdom
Crabtree Publishing
Maritime House
Basin Road North, Hove
BN41 1WR

Published in Australia
Crabtree Publishing
3 Charles Street
Coburg North
VIC 3058

Contents

Animal challenges

*The Yunnan snub-nosed monkey was so rare, scientists thought it was **extinct** until the 1960s! What challenges do they face today? (See page 12.)*

***Climate change** is making it harder for polar bears and other animals to survive (see pages 24–25).*

Thousands of **species**, or types, of animals face huge challenges. Many are endangered. Forest animals often lose their habitats because their forest homes are cut down or burned to be replaced by farms or cities. Some are hunted for food or body parts such as their meat, skin, or tusks. Still others are caught to be sold as pets or used to entertain tourists. Animals that live in oceans also face big challenges. Many penguins, seabirds, sharks, whales, sea turtles, and fish are endangered because of thoughtless human activities.

This brown bear has caught a salmon that was swimming toward the ocean. How does raising salmon for food hurt wild salmon and the animals that depend on them for food? (See pages 26–27.)

How is tourism hurting wild animals such as dolphins, orcas, and sea turtles? (See page 22.)

Why is it dangerous for gorillas to be near people? (See page 14.)

What dangers do sea turtles face at night? (See page 23.)

Forest fires

Slash-and-burn agriculture is a way of growing food in which forests are cut down and burned so the land can be used to grow crops. The fires often burn out of control. Slash-and-burn agriculture is practiced in the Amazon Rainforest, as well as in Africa and Southeast Asia. In 2015, thousands of small forest fires burned across the islands of Indonesia in Southeast Asia. Fires release huge amounts of pollution into the atmosphere. This makes breathing difficult and is very dangerous to the health of humans and animals. The carbon dioxide it releases also adds to climate change.

Forest fires not only destroy the habitats of many animals, but they also cause animals to die from the smoke. Fires may cause many critically endangered animals to disappear from Earth (see pages 8–9).

Palm oil

Slash-and-burn fires are set on purpose to replace forests with farms and palm-oil plantations. Palm oil is used in many foods such as ice cream, margarine, soups, and cookies. It is also found in makeup, soap, and detergents.

kernel   pulp

Palm oil is made from palm fruits like these. They are gathered, and the oil is extracted, or drawn out, from both the pulp and the kernels.

This man is collecting palm fruits from the trees in a palm-oil plantation in Thailand.

Animals in trouble

Some of Earth's most endangered animals, such as Sumatran tigers and elephants, as well as Sumatran and Bornean orangutans, are at risk from the huge fires in Indonesia. Many animals have died from the smoke and fire. As forest fires destroy animal habitats across Indonesia, Malaysia, Singapore, Thailand, and other nearby countries, wild animals are forced to move into farm areas and towns to find food. When wild animals come too close to people's homes, both humans and animals may die. People shoot tigers because they are afraid for their lives and for the lives of their farm animals. They kill elephants and orangutans to keep them from eating their food.

Baby orangutans become ill from inhaling smoke from fires, just as human babies do. These sick baby orangutans were taken to a shelter by an animal rescue group.

Sumatran tigers and elephants have fled burning rain forests and moved toward farms and villages. Tigers often kill farm animals and people while they hunt at night. Elephants eat some of the food that farmers grow. Both of these endangered animals are being trapped and killed by people.

What do you think?

When wild animals lose their homes, they often move into towns, cities, or onto farmlands. Have any wild animals moved into your neighborhood? Why? What problems have they caused in your community?

Sumatran elephant

9

Endemic island animals

An island is an area of land that has water all around it. Islands are found all over the world in oceans, rivers, and lakes. New Guinea is a large island near Australia, and Madagascar is a big island that is part of Africa. The state of Hawaii and the country of Indonesia are each made up of many islands. Many kinds of animals that live on islands are **endemic**. Endemic animals live only in certain places in the world. Many endemic animals are critically endangered because, when they die out, they will not be found anywhere else on Earth. Endemic island animals face some of the biggest challenges from habitat loss, hunting, and forest fires. All the animals on pages 8 to 11 are endemic island animals.

*The fossa is the largest **carnivore** of the mammals on Madagascar. It is the size of a small cougar. Lemurs are the fossa's main food. As their forest habitats disappear, the number of lemurs is decreasing. Without enough food, fossas cannot survive.*

This island fox is endemic to San Miguel, one of the Channel Islands in California. It became critically endangered because wild pigs, which were brought to the island, ate its food, and golden eagles hunted it. People have worked hard to increase the numbers of this fox in its habitat.

The Hawaiian monk seal is the only seal endemic to the Hawaiian islands. It is critically endangered. Monk seals get tangled up in fishing gear and are often attacked by sharks. Climate change is another challenge they face. As sea levels rise, there is less land for the seals to use for resting and having babies.

Island homes

Which of the animals shown here are losing their habitats? Why do monk seals need to be on beaches as well as in the ocean? Which animal is in danger of losing the main food it eats?

Most tree kangaroos live in Australia, but the Huon tree kangaroo lives on the island of New Guinea. A lot of the trees on which these kangaroos live are being cut down. The kangaroos are also threatened by people who hunt them for their meat and fur.

11

Snub-nosed monkeys

Yunnan monkeys have bright red lips and a crown of black hair on their heads. With less than 2,000 left, China has created a program to protect them.

Sichuan golden monkey with baby

Yunnan snub-nosed monkeys live in the highest forests in the world, located in the mountains of southwest China. Their habitats are higher than those of any other primates, except humans. Yunnan monkeys are called "mystery monkeys" because, until the 1960s, people had not seen them for more than 100 years. These monkeys live in **troops** and travel around their habitat together.

Golden monkeys

The first snub-nosed monkeys to be discovered were Sichuan golden monkeys. They have thick orange hair and long tails. These monkeys also live in mountain forests in central and southwest China and can survive in cold temperatures and snow. They spend most of their time in the treetops.

Tonkin snub-nosed monkeys live only in Vietnam. They are critically endangered because of habitat loss and hunting.

Endangered monkeys

Other snub-nosed monkeys are Myanmar snub-nosed monkeys, gray snub-nosed monkeys, and Tonkin monkeys. They all live in mountain forests, and all are endangered. The Tonkin monkeys, shown above, have the smallest population. There are only about 200 of these monkeys left.

Monkey challenges

Like other animals, monkeys are losing their habitats and are being hunted. Some monkeys are not afraid of people and are eating the foods that people give them, which are not as nutritious as the natural foods that they find for themselves.

Catching diseases

These tourists might make this orangutan sick.

The body structures and **genes** of chimpanzees, gorillas, orangutans, and people are closely related. All these species can become ill from more than 140 of the same diseases. **Ebola** has killed about one-third of western lowland gorillas. As more gorillas lose their habitats, more will have contact with humans.

This baby gorilla does not feel well. What made it sick?

Challenges from people

Park rangers, soldiers, and tourists often come too close to apes and pass on diseases that could kill them. Measles, influenza, and tuberculosis are dangerous diseases that are often passed to apes by people who live nearby. Local people also endanger gorillas and chimpanzees when they hunt them illegally for their meat.

Trapping pets

Many kinds of monkeys and apes are trapped to be sold as pets because people think they are cute. When baby monkeys or apes are taken from their mothers, they are often sad and do not survive. Monkeys are very social animals and need their family groups. Living with people is a big challenge for these animals!

Langur babies need their mothers to care for them and teach them skills. Baby Douc langurs, above, and Francois's langurs, below, are popular as pets, even though it is illegal to own either one.

For each baby orangutan that is captured, it is estimated that six to eight orangutans die. The mothers are shot, and many babies die while they are transported to where they will be sold.

Capuchin monkeys, right, are very smart. They can be trained to do tasks for people who do not have use of their arms or legs. People also keep them as pets, but they are not easy to look after.

15

Sound pollution

Sonar is a series of pulsing sounds used by navies to find objects, such as submarines, in the ocean. The sound waves can travel across hundreds of miles of ocean and drown out the noises that ocean animals make for their survival. Dolphins and whales use sounds to find food, friends, and mates. Loud sonar noises can keep ocean animals from noticing ships coming toward them. They can strike whales with great force and even cause their death.

The force of sonar vibrations can shock whales and cause them to leap out of the water too quickly and too high. Coming up too quickly creates bleeding in their brains and large air bubbles in their organs, causing death.

Sonar can cause whales to become confused and to swim away from the sound. They may not know which way they are going and become stranded on land or in shallow water. Once stranded, they cannot move to get back into the ocean. This humpback whale was found stranded on a beach. People tried to help the whale, but it was too late. They left flowers to show that they cared.

Oil rigs and spills

Noises from oil-drilling **rigs**, or equipment, can also cause marine mammals to become confused. Oil spills can clog the blowholes through which whales and dolphins breathe and cause them to suffocate. After an oil spill, it is difficult for many ocean animals to have babies.

oil rig

Seabirds in danger

The coastlines and islands along the southern tip of South America have the largest breeding colonies for albatrosses and Magellanic penguins. The bodies of many seabirds have been found washed up along these coasts. The challenges these birds face include oil spills, pollution, poisons, and diseases. Some baby penguins were also found born without feathers. Without feathers, penguins cannot survive the cold.

Magellanic penguins build nests in burrows on beaches. Climate change has caused smaller fish populations, so penguins must swim much farther to find food. The parents take turns caring for the chicks and going fishing. The chicks and the parent in the nest often starve before the other parent can bring food.

Another challenge for penguin chicks is tourists. Newly hatched chicks become stressed because of the number of times they get visited and handled. People find them fascinating, but it is too much for baby birds that need to get used to their new world.

The population of black-browed albatrosses has declined more than 60 percent in South America because of the fishing practices of people. The birds often become trapped in fishing nets and die. They also die from different diseases and poisons found in the ocean.

Hunters and poachers

African elephants are in grave danger from **poachers**. Poachers are illegal hunters who kill animals for their body parts, such as elephant tusks. Elephant tusks are taken for their **ivory**, a hard white material from which many kinds of objects are made. Elephants live in social groups called herds. When a member of a herd dies, the other elephants mourn the death for many days. Many baby elephants lose their mothers when they are killed by poachers for their tusks.

The picture on the left shows elephant tusks that were taken from poachers. Tusks are often used to make works of art, such as the statue on the right.

Young elephants whose mothers have been killed are often very sad and need someone to be with them night and day. People who rescue elephants feed them milk from bottles and often sleep near them.

Entertaining tourists

People love swimming with dolphins and watching orcas, the biggest dolphins, perform in shows. Taking dolphins and orcas from their pods in the ocean, however, changes the lives of the captive animals, as well as those of their pods. Orcas travel up to 100 miles (160 km) a day, so living in swimming pools is like being in prison. The animals are too big and intelligent for captivity. Captive orcas have hurt and even killed some of their trainers because they feel stressed. Wild orcas in oceans live 50 to 90 years, but captive dolphins often die before the age of five.

Orca babies born in captivity often die soon after birth. In the wild, orcas stay with their families. In captivity, families are split apart.

Turtle troubles

Sea turtles live in oceans, but to lay their eggs, adult females must go ashore to make nests. Each female swims to the beach where she hatched from an egg. Some swim thousands of miles! When the turtle has finished laying her eggs at night, she drags herself across the sand toward the ocean.

How might this sign help nesting sea turtles?

Going toward light

The sky looks bright over water, so the turtle heads toward the light. However, most of the light today comes from hotels built on the beaches where turtles nest. Confused, the turtles often go the wrong way. After hatching, baby sea turtles head for the ocean, but they often make the same mistake.

This leatherback sea turtle is going toward the light, but is the light coming from a hotel?

Will these babies make it to the ocean?

23

Climate change

Earth's climate is changing. Warmer temperatures are causing the usual sea ice on which polar bears eat to disappear during the summer and form later in the fall. The bears hunt seals and fish in the water and drag them onto the sea ice to eat them. The food builds up a bear's body fat, giving it energy. Less sea ice makes it harder for polar bears to hunt. If they do not catch enough food, their health suffers, especially bears that are nursing cubs. The main cause of death in cubs occurs when their mothers cannot make enough milk to feed them.

Polar bear mothers need fat to make milk so they can nurse their cubs. As they get bigger, the cubs also need the meat their mothers hunt.

Golden toads gone!

The golden toad once lived in mountaintop forests in Costa Rica. Higher temperatures and less rainfall changed their habitat, causing the toads to die off. The golden toad is now extinct, which means there are no more of them left on Earth.

Hundreds of golden toads used to breed in small pools in the rainy season, but their habitat is too dry for these toads to exist today.

Endangered whales

The North Atlantic right whale is one of the most endangered of all large whales. Only about 400 of these whales are alive on Earth today. Right whales spend part of the year feeding in colder waters before migrating to warm waters to have their calves. As ocean temperatures get warmer, there is less food for the whales to eat before they migrate and give birth.

*Before they migrate from their feeding grounds, female whales must eat a lot to add **blubber**, or fat, to their bodies. They need plenty of blubber to stay alive and make enough milk to feed their calves.*

Fishing and fish farming

Wild salmon spend their early lives in rivers and then swim out to oceans as adults. They return to the rivers to lay their eggs. As they swim past salmon farms, they pick up diseases and sea lice.

A new kind of salmon is now being raised, which grows much faster and bigger than wild salmon. It eats much more food, so if it escaped, it would outcompete the wild salmon populations for food.

Today, most of the salmon we eat are raised in fish farms. Salmon farming is harmful to wild salmon, as well as to people. The fish are raised in open cages placed in the ocean, where chemicals, **sea lice**, and pesticides can often be found in the water. These are absorbed by the fish and eaten by humans. Penned up in a small area, the fish also create a lot of waste, which can harm other ocean animals, such as seals and dolphins.

salmon cages

Fishing dangers

People use different ways to catch fish. Each type of fishing poses dangers to ocean habitats and the animals that live in them. Gillnets, for example, are used to catch sardines, salmon, and cod, but can accidentally trap and kill other animals, such as the moray eel, shown on the right. Trawling, another way of fishing, drags huge nets along the bottom of the ocean.

A bottom trawl is a type of fishing net that is pulled along the seafloor by one or two small open boats or a large ship. This picture shows two boats about to trawl together to catch shrimp and fish that live near the bottom of the ocean. Besides these fish, however, the nets might accidentally catch sea turtles or dolphins. These animals are often thrown back dead or dying. Dragging heavy nets across the bottom of the ocean can also damage ocean-floor habitats, such as coral reefs.

Back home again

black-footed ferret

prairie dog

Some animals, such as the black-footed ferret and the blue iguana became extinct in the wild but were saved from dying out completely. The remaining animals were bred in captivity and introduced back into their wild habitats. More than 1,000 black-footed ferrets now live in some prairie habitats in parts of Canada and the United States.

Black-footed ferrets are once again hunting prairie dogs, as they did in the past. They were brought to places where they could find plenty of prairie dogs to hunt so they would survive.

Blue iguanas back in the wild

Blue iguanas once lived along the coasts and in other areas of Grand Cayman, a large Caribbean island. By 2002, they had become critically endangered. The lizard's numbers decreased to between 5 and 25 because of habitat loss and being hit by cars. Dogs and cats also ate these lizards. The Blue Iguana Recovery Program was created to breed, care for, and release hundreds of these iguanas back into protected wild areas. They are now growing in numbers.

Blue iguanas grow to be 5 feet (1.5 m) long. They are the largest land animals on Grand Cayman. Young iguanas, like the two above, are brown.

29

How you can help

Almost every challenge that animals face is caused by humans. Forest fires, hunting and poaching, trapping pets, pollution, fishing, and climate change are just some of the big challenges that animals face today. There are many things you can do to help. One of the best things you can do is to learn more about these animals and what they need. You can also teach others what you have learned.

*Ask your parents to buy more **organic** and fewer **processed** foods. While shopping, make a list of foods that contain palm oil. Then share the list with your classmates and discuss the damage that palm-oil plantations create.*

What can you teach others about helping animals?

What are your challenges?

Do you live in an area that has challenging weather or forest fires? Which animal challenges are like yours? How are they the same and different?

Videos and films

Watching a video or documentary about animal challenges will help you see and understand the big problems animals face. Ask your teacher or parent to help you find documentaries or videos about animals such as elephants, polar bears, and whales. These videos will get you started.

Mission: Polar Bear Rescue
http://kids.nationalgeographic.com/
videos/mission-animal-rescue/
#mission_animal_rescue_polar_
bears.mp4

Mission: Elephant Rescue
http://kids.nationalgeographic.com/
videos/mission-animal-rescue/
#mission_animal_rescue_
elephants.mp4

Orangutan rescue
http://natgeotv.com/asia/orangutan-
rescue/videos/baby-orangutan-school

Become an Earth Ranger!
Find out how kids can help animals at www.earthrangers.com

Amazing whale! We see your tail above the shining sea.
We send you love and healing, too.
We are your family.

Write your own poem about whales to show that you care about them.

This baby elephant is being fed milk from a bottle at a shelter after its mother was killed by poachers.

31

Glossary

Note: Some boldfaced words are defined where they appear in the book.

breeding colony An area where animals of the same species mate, give birth, and raise their young

carnivore An animal that eats other animals

climate change A change in the long-term weather conditions on Earth, often due to an increase in average temperature

Ebola A deadly disease that causes high fevers and bleeding inside the body

endemic Belonging or found only in a certain area

extinct Describing a plant or an animal that has died out or is no longer found in the wild

gene A part of a cell in the body that is responsible for passing on characteristics from one generation to another

organic Referring to plants or animals grown or raised without the use of artifical ingredients

processed Referring to something that has been put through a special process in order to change or perserve it

sea lice Small animals found in water that attach and feed off fish

sonar An instrument that sends out radio waves to discover and locate objects under the water

troop The social group of apes and monkeys

Index